The Cherry Orchard

Plays

Rosencrantz and Guildenstern Are Dead ★
Enter a Free Man ★ • The Real Inspector Hound ★
After Magritte ★ • Jumpers ★ • Travesties ★
Dirty Linen and New-Found-Land ★
Every Good Boy Deserves Favour ★
Night and Day • Dogg's Hamlet, Cahoot's Macbeth ★
Undiscovered Country
(adapted from Arthur Schnitzler's Das weite Land)
On the Razzle
(adapted from Johann Nestroy's Einen Jux will er sich machen)
The Real Thing • Rough Crossing
(adapted from Ferenc Molnár's Play at the Castle)
Dalliance (adapted from Arthur Schnitzler's Liebelei)
Hapgood • Arcadia
Indian Ink (an adaptation of In the Native State)
The Invention of Love ★ • Voyage: The Coast of Utopia Part I ★
Shipwreck: The Coast of Utopia Part II ★
Salvage: The Coast of Utopia Part III ★
Rock 'n' Roll ★

Television Scripts
A Separate Peace • Teeth • Another Moon Called Earth
Neutral Ground • Professional Foul • Squaring the Circle

Radio Plays
The Dissolution of Dominic Boot
"M" Is for Moon Among Other Things
If You're Glad, I'll Be Frank • Albert's Bridge
Where Are They Now? • Artist Descending a Staircase
The Dog It Was That Died • In the Native State
On Dover Beach

Screenplays
Rosencrantz and Guildenstern Are Dead
Shakespeare in Love (with Marc Norman)

Fiction
Lord Malquist and Mr. Moon★

★Available from Grove Press

The Cherry Orchard
A Comedy in Four Acts

BY
ANTON CHEKHOV

ENGLISH VERSION
BY TOM STOPPARD

From a Literal Translation by Helen Rappaport

Grove Press
New York

Printed in the United States of America

ISBN: 978-0-8021-4409-6

Grove Press
an imprint of Grove/Atlantic, Inc.
154 West 14th Street
New York, NY 10011

Distributed by Publishers Group West

www.groveatlantic.com

Tom Stoppard's English version of *The Cherry Orchard* by Anton Chekhov had its first performance at the Brooklyn Academy of Music's Harvey Theater, Brooklyn, New York, on 2 January 2009, and its UK premiere at The Old Vic Theatre, London, on 23 May 2009 and was presented by The Bridge Project, a collaboration of the Brooklyn Academy of Music, The Old Vic, and Neal Street Productions.

The cast in order of appearance was as follows:

DUNYASHA   Charlotte Parry
LOPAKHIN   Simon Russell Beale
YEPIKHODOV   Tobias Segal
ANYA   Morven Christie
RANEVSKAYA   Sinéad Cusack
VARYA   Rebecca Hall
GAEV   Paul Jesson
CHARLOTTA IVANOVNA   Selina Cadell
SIMEONOV-PISHCHIK   Dakin Matthews
YASHA   Josh Hamilton
FIRS   Richard Easton
TROFIMOV   Ethan Hawke
PASSER-BY   Gary Powell
STATION MASTER   Mark Nelson
POST OFFICE CLERK   Aaron Krohn
GUESTS, SERVANTS   Michael Braun, Aaron Krohn, Jessica Pollert Smith, and Hannah Stokely

Director   Sam Mendes
Set design   Anthony Ward
Costume design   Catherine Zuber
Lighting design   Paul Pyant
Sound design   Paul Arditti
Music   Mark Bennett

THE
CHERRY ORCHARD

LIST OF CHARACTERS

RANEVSKAYA, Liubov Andreevna, a landowner

ANYA, her daughter, seventeen years old

VARYA, her adopted daughter, twenty-four years old

GAEV, Leonid Andreevich, Ranevskaya's brother

LOPAKHIN, Yermolai Alekseevich, a businessman

TROFIMOV, Pyotr Sergeevich, a student

SIMEONOV-PISHCHIK, Boris Borisovich, a landowner

CHARLOTTA IVANOVNA, a governess

YEPIKHODOV, Semyon Panteleevich, a clerk

DUNYASHA, a housemaid

FIRS, a manservant, eighty-seven years old

YASHA, a young manservant

PASSER-BY

STATION MASTER

POST OFFICE CLERK

GUESTS, SERVANTS

ACT ONE

A room which is still called the nursery. One of the doors leads into Anya's room. Daybreak, just before sunrise. It is May but still cold, with a morning frost. LOPAKHIN has fallen asleep over a book. A train is approaching at a distance, slowing down. It gets closer and louder, still slowing. At its closest approach, not proximate, Lopakhin stirs, still asleep. The book falls from his lap. Still slowing but receding now, the train gives a quite distant warning whistle of imminent arrival. Lopakhin wakes, collecting himself, then cross with himself. The train is no longer heard. DUNYASHA enters, surprised to see Lopakhin there.

DUNYASHA I thought you'd gone to the station.

LOPAKHIN Thank God the train's in at last. What time is it?

DUNYASHA Nearly two (*she blows out the candle*) It's already light.

LOPAKHIN So it's, what, two hours late. More. (*he yawns and stretches*) Well, what a fool I am. Came all this way specially to meet them off the train, and fell asleep sitting here. You should have woken me.

DUNYASHA I thought you'd gone.

Pause.

LOPAKHIN (*pensive*) Liubov Andreevna Ranevskaya . . .

Pause.

LOPAKHIN (*cont.*) I wonder what she's like now after five years living abroad. She's a good woman. An easy, straightforward sort of person. Once, when I was just a kid, fifteen or so, my father, he's dead now but he used to have

3

a shop in the village, well, he thumped me in the face, my nose was bleeding like a tap. We'd come into the yard out there (*he gestures*) for some reason, and he was drunk. Liubov Andreevna—I can see her now, she was a skinny little thing when she was young—she brought me indoors, into this very room, it was the nursery. She takes me over to the washstand. "Don't cry, little peasant," she says, "it'll be better in time for your wedding."

Pause.

LOPAKHIN (*cont.*) "Little peasant." Son of a peasant, true enough, and here I am in a white waistcoat and fancy shoes like a pig in a parlour, only rich, with money to spend but look twice and I'm still a peasant to a peasant. (*he picks up the book*) I was reading this book, couldn't understand a word of it. I fell asleep over it.

DUNYASHA I think they're here.

LOPAKHIN (*listens*) No, there'll be bags to get down and all that sort of thing.

Pause.

DUNYASHA The dogs were stirring all night—they know the mistress is coming.

LOPAKHIN Are you all right, Dunyasha?—you're . . .

DUNYASHA My hands won't stop shaking. I feel as if I'm going to swoon.

LOPAKHIN You're too sensitive for your own good. You dress up like a lady, and look at your hair. It won't do. You want to remember where you come from.

4

Enter YEPIKHODOV *with a bunch of flowers. He wears a jacket and brightly polished boots that squeak loudly. As he enters, he drops a few flowers clumsily.*

YEPIKHODOV (*picking up the flowers*)   For the dining-room— the gardener sent them in.

He hands Dunyasha the flowers.

LOPAKHIN (*to Dunyasha*)   And bring me some kvass, would you?

DUNYASHA (*going out*)   Yes, sir.

YEPIKHODOV   Three degrees of frost and the cherry trees in blossom—I don't call that a climate, I mean really, the seasons get no cooperation at all. And while I'm on the subject, I bought these boots three days ago and they squeak, see for yourself, there's nothing to be done with them, I mean, what can I grease them with?

LOPAKHIN   Give it a rest, you're getting on my nerves.

YEPIKHODOV   Every day there's something, some misfortune. But do I complain? I do not. I'm used to it. Keep smiling, that's me.

Dunyasha enters, and gives Lopakhin the kvass.

YEPIKHODOV   I'll be off then.

He stumbles into a chair, which falls over.

YEPIKHODOV (*cont.*)   There, you see! (*triumphant*) See what I mean? What a circumstancive situation if I say so myself. It's uncanny.

Yepikhodov goes out.

DUNYASHA Shall I tell you something?—he's proposed to me, Yepikhodov has!

LOPAKHIN Has he!

DUNYASHA I don't know what to think. He's normally the quiet type but now and again when he gets to talking he doesn't make a lot of sense. He talks very nice and you can tell he means it but you can't understand what he's on about. I even quite like him, I think. He's mad about me! But he's an unlucky sort of person, things keep happening to him. The servants call him Catastrophe Corner.

LOPAKHIN (*listening*) I think they're coming.

DUNYASHA They're here! What's the matter with me? I'm shivering.

LOPAKHIN Yes, that's them. We should go and meet them. I wonder if she'll recognize me, it's been five years. . . .

DUNYASHA (*agitated*) I'm going to faint away!—I am, I'm going to faint!

Two carriages can be heard drawing up to the house. Lopakhin and Dunyasha hurry out. The stage is empty. Noises off. FIRS, who has been to meet the train, hurriedly crosses the stage, leaning on a stick. He is wearing ancient livery and a top hat. He is muttering inaudibly. The noise off-stage increases.

ANYA'S VOICE We can go through here.

A crowd of people enter and cross the stage: LIUBOV ANDREEVNA, ANYA and CHARLOTTA IVANOVNA, who has a small dog on a lead, all dressed for travelling; VARYA in an overcoat and kerchief, GAEV, SIMEONOV-PISHCHIK, Lopakhin, Dunyasha, with a bundle and an umbrella, and servants with luggage, etc.

ANYA Do you remember what room this is, Mama?

LIUBOV (*joyfully, on the brink of tears*) The nursery!

VARYA It's so cold. My hands are numb. (*to Liubov Andreevna*) We've kept your rooms just as they were, Mama—the white room and the lavender room, do you remember?

LIUBOV The nursery . . . ! My dear beautiful nursery. This is where I used to sleep when I was little . . . (*weeping now*) I'm a little girl again . . . (*she kisses her brother, Gaev, and her adopted daughter, Varya, then Gaev again*) Varya hasn't changed at all, you still look like a nun. And I know *you*, Dunyasha . . . (*she kisses Dunyasha*).

GAEV The train was two hours late. Just think of it! They need to get themselves organised.

CHARLOTTA (*to Pishchik*) This dog eats nuts.

PISHCHIK (*amazed*) Really? Fancy that!

Everyone continues out except Anya and Dunyasha.

DUNYASHA We waited and waited till we thought you'd never come.

Dunyasha takes off Anya's coat and hat.

ANYA I didn't sleep for four nights on the train. I'm frozen stiff.

DUNYASHA When you set off in Lent it was all snow and ice—but now look! (*laughs, kisses her*) I've been waiting for you, my lovely, my precious, I have to tell you, I can't wait another minute . . .

ANYA (*tiredly*) What now?

DUNYASHA Yepikhodov the clerk, straight after Easter, he proposed to me!

ANYA That's all you ever think about. (*tidying her hair*) I've lost all my hairpins one by one.

She is almost staggering with exhaustion.

DUNYASHA I just don't know *what* to think. He's terribly in love with me.

ANYA (*looks through her doorway, tenderly*) Oh, my room, my windows . . . ! As though I've never been away. Home at last! When I wake up I'm going to go straight out into the garden. If only I could get to sleep! The whole way here I was so worried I never slept at all.

DUNYASHA Trofimov's come back.

ANYA (*joyfully*) Petya's here?

DUNYASHA The day before yesterday. He's asleep in the bathhouse—he's moved in there. He says he doesn't want to be in the way. (*looking at her pocket watch*) I ought to wake him up, but Varya said not to. Don't you go waking him, she said.

Enter Varya. On her belt she has a bunch of keys.

VARYA Mama's asking for coffee—quick as you can, Dunyasha.

DUNYASHA Coming, coming!

She goes out.

VARYA Well, you're here at last, thank the Lord—home again. (*cuddles her*) My little one is home—my darling.

ANYA What I've been through since I saw you!

VARYA   I can just imagine!

ANYA   It was so cold when I left in Easter week. Charlotta talked the whole way and never left off with her conjuring tricks. Why ever did you have to stick me with her?

VARYA   My darling, you can't go travelling on your own at seventeen.

ANYA   Anyway, we get to Paris and it's so cold. It's snowing. My French is hopeless. Mama's living five floors up. So I arrive and she's got some French people with her, some ladies, and an old Catholic priest mumbling over a book. It was horribly crowded with everybody smoking. All of a sudden I felt so sorry for Mama, I put my arms around her head and hugged her tight, I couldn't let go, and then she was kissing me and crying . . .

VARYA   (*fighting back tears*)   Don't . . . don't . . .

ANYA   The villa near Menton is already sold. She has nothing left, nothing at all. I haven't got a kopek, we barely made it to Paris. And Mama simply doesn't take it in. At the station restaurant she ordered the most expensive things on the menu and tipped the waiters a rouble each. Charlotta's the same. And Yasha orders for himself, it's just awful. Yasha is Mama's footman now, we brought him back with us.

VARYA   I saw him, the good-for-nothing.

ANYA   So, what's happening?—has the interest been paid?

VARYA   With what?

ANYA   Oh God, please God . . .

VARYA   The whole estate's going to be sold by August.

ANYA   Oh God . . . !

Lopakhin looks in, moos, and disappears.

VARYA (*on the brink of tears*)   Oh, I'd like to . . .

Varya makes a fist. Anya embraces her gently.

ANYA   Varya, has he proposed yet?

Varya shakes her head.

ANYA (*cont.*)   But it's obvious he loves you. Why can't the two of you come to an understanding? What are you waiting for?

VARYA   If you want to know what I think, nothing's going to come of it. He's busy with his affairs, he hasn't got time. He doesn't take any notice of me. Well, good luck to him. I don't want to see him, it just makes me unhappy. People keep talking about our marriage, some of them even congratulate me, but it's all built on nothing, it's all a fantasy. (*with a change of tone*) Oh—you're wearing a new brooch, it's a bumble bee.

ANYA (*despairing*)   Mama just had to buy it for me.

Anya goes into her room, talking cheerfully, a child again.

ANYA (*cont.*)   In Paris I went up in a hot-air balloon!

VARYA (*laughs happily*)   Now I know you're back! My Anya is home!

Dunyasha has returned with a coffee pot and is pouring the coffee. Varya talks to Anya through the door.

VARYA (*cont.*)   All day long while I'm seeing to the house, I'm racking my brains. If only we could get you married off to some rich man, it would be such a weight off my mind. I could disappear into a retreat somewhere, disappear further and further, to Kiev, to Moscow. I'd go on a pilgrimage around all the holy places, I'd walk forever, oh, what a glorious thought!

ANYA   The birds are singing in the orchard! What time is it?

VARYA   It must be well after two. Bedtime for you, my pet.

She follows Anya into her room.

VARYA (*cont.*)   . . . Yes . . . what a glorious thought.

YASHA *enters with a rug and a travelling bag, and crosses the stage with exaggerated discretion.*

YASHA   May one intrude?—just passing through.

DUNYASHA   I wouldn't have known you, Yasha. Abroad has changed you.

YASHA   Oh yes?—and who might you be?

DUNYASHA   When you left I was so-high . . . (*indicating height from the floor*) Dunyasha, Fyodor Kozoedov's daughter. You don't remember!

YASHA   Ah yes . . . and ripe for plucking!

Yasha looks around and then puts his arms around her; she shrieks and drops a saucer. Yasha hurries out.

VARYA (*in the doorway, irritably*)   What's going on?

DUNYASHA (*on the brink of tears*)   I've broken a saucer . . .

VARYA   It's good luck.

ANYA (*coming out of her room*)   We should warn Mama about Petya being here . . .

VARYA   It's all right—I told them not to wake him.

ANYA (*reflectively*) Six years since Papa died, and my little brother drowned in the river barely a month after, little Grisha, only seven and so pretty. It was too much for Mama. She left and didn't look back, she just ran and ran. (*shudders*) I understand her so well. If only she knew. (*pause*) It might bring it all back, seeing Grisha's tutor again.

Enter Firs; he's in a jacket and white waistcoat. He goes to the coffee pot, preoccupied.

FIRS The mistress will be taking her coffee in here . . . (*putting on white gloves*) Is it ready? (*to Dunyasha, sternly*) Where's the cream?—wake up, girl!

DUNYASHA Oh!—oh, my goodness . . .

Dunyasha rushes out.

FIRS (*dealing with the coffee pot*) You noodle . . . (*mutters to himself*) They've come all the way from Paris. The master went to Paris in his coach once. (*laughs*)

VARYA Firs, what are you muttering about?

FIRS What is it? (*joyfully*) The mistress is home! The long wait is over! I don't mind if I die now . . . (*weeps with joy*) Now it's all right to die.

Enter Liubov Andreevna, Lopakhin, Gaev, and Simeonov-Pishchik, who is wearing a long, tight-fitting coat of fine cloth and loose Turkish trousers. Gaev, as he comes in, plays air billiards.

LIUBOV How does it go?—Let's see—I pot the yellow into the corner pocket—and go off the cushion into the middle.

GAEV Screw-shot into the top corner! We used to sleep in this room once upon a time, my little sister and I, and now I'm fifty-one years old, hard to believe.

LOPAKHIN   Yes, time passes.

GAEV   What?

LOPAKHIN   Time. I said it passes.

GAEV   It smells of cheap scent in here.

ANYA   I'm going to bed. (*kissing her mother*) Goodnight Mama.

LIUBOV   My little baby. (*kisses her hands*) Are you glad to be home? I can't quite believe it.

ANYA   Goodnight, uncle.

GAEV (*kisses her face and hands*)   God bless you. You're so like your mother! (*to his sister*) Liuba, you were so like her at her age.

Anya gives her hand to Lopakhin and Pishchik, goes out and closes the door behind her.

LIUBOV   She's tired out.

PISHCHIK   Well, a long journey, of course . . .

VARYA (*to Lopakhin and Pishchik*)   So, gentlemen, long past two and time to be going.

LIUBOV (*laughs*)   Same old Varya. (*draws her close and kisses her*) I'll have my coffee and then we'll all go. (*Firs puts a cushion under her feet*) Thank you, you're a dear. I've got used to having my coffee, I drink it day and night. Thank you, my dear old friend. (*kisses Firs*)

VARYA   I'll go and see that they've brought everything in.

Varya goes out.

LIUBOV   Am I really here? Is this me? (*laughs*) I feel like dancing about and swinging my arms around. (*covers her face with her hands*) Perhaps it's all a dream. God knows I love my country, I love it so dearly. I couldn't see out of the train window, I was crying so much. (*on the brink of tears*) Well, I must drink my coffee. Thank you, Firs, thank you, you dear old man, I'm so glad you didn't die.

FIRS The day before yesterday.

GAEV His hearing's gone.

LOPAKHIN I've got to leave for Kharkov soon, by the early train—it's a nuisance. I was looking forward to seeing you and having a talk—you still look as wonderful as ever.

PISHCHIK (*breathing heavily*) More than ever . . . dressed in the latest Paris fashions. You could tip my cart wheels-up!

LOPAKHIN Your brother here thinks I'm vulgar, a jumped-up kulak, but I don't care, he can think what he likes, all I care is that you trust me as you used to—and when you look at me with those heartbreaking eyes you see me as you always did. Merciful God—my father was a serf in your father's time, and before that he belonged to your grandfather, but you—you alone—you were always so good to me that I no longer think about that, and I love you like my own flesh and blood . . . more than my flesh and blood.

LIUBOV I can't sit still—my body won't let me.

Liubov leaps up and walks up and down, in a great agitation.

LIUBOV (*cont.*) I could die with happiness, I'm silly with it and you can laugh at me. Here's my little book cupboard!— (*kissing the book cupboard*) and my little table . . .

GAEV Nanny died while you were away.

Liubov sits down and sips her coffee.

LIUBOV I know, God rest her. They wrote to me.

GAEV And Anastasii died . . . Pyotr the squint has left—he's in town in the police office now.

He takes a box of lemon drops out of his pocket and sucks one.

PISHCHIK My daughter Dashenka asks to be remembered.

LOPAKHIN Look, there's something I came to tell you, something nice, to cheer you up. (*looking at his watch*) I haven't got much time to go into it, I have to leave soon, but, well, all right, I'll make it quick. As you know only too well, the cherry orchard is to be sold off against your debts, the auction is fixed for the 22nd of August—but you needn't distress yourself, my dear, you can sleep easy, because there is a way out. Here's what I've thought of, listen carefully. Your estate is only a dozen miles from town, the new railway branch runs alongside it, and if the cherry orchard and the land along the river were divided up into lots for leasing out for summer cottages, you'd end up with an income of at least twenty-five thousand roubles a year.

GAEV Excuse me, but what is this nonsense!

LIUBOV I don't understand what you mean.

LOPAKHIN People will pay at least twenty-five roubles a year for the building plots, and if you advertise now I'll bet you anything you like that by August there won't be a plot left, they'll be snapped up. In a word—congratulations. You're saved. It's a beautiful situation, the river is deep enough for swimming—

A miss-step; he recovers almost instantly.

LOPAKHIN (*cont.*)   All you have to do is clear the ground, tidy it up, get rid of the old buildings, like this house, which won't have any use now, and cut down the cherry orchard!

LIUBOV   Cut it down? My dear, I'm sorry but you don't understand. If there's one thing of any interest—one remarkable feature—in this whole district, it's our cherry orchard.

LOPAKHIN   The only remarkable thing about your cherry orchard is it's big. But it only gives a crop every other year, and then you don't know what to do with all the cherries, no one wants to buy them.

GAEV   Our cherry orchard is mentioned in the encyclopaedia.

LOPAKHIN (*glancing at his watch*)   If we don't come up with something and make a decision, on the 22nd of August it won't just be the cherry orchard on the block, it'll be the whole estate. You have to face up to it. Believe me, there's no other way out, there absolutely isn't.

FIRS   In the old days, forty, fifty years ago, they dried the cherries, then soaked them, pickled them, made jam out of them, and sometimes they—

GAEV   Yes, all right, Firs.

FIRS   Back then, the dried cherries were sent off in cartloads to Moscow and Kharkov. There was money in them back then! And your dried cherry isn't what it used to be—they were soft and juicy, sweet, with a fragrance to them, they knew how to do it, they had the secret.

LIUBOV   And where is the secret now?

FIRS   Forgotten. No one remembers it.

PISHCHIK (*to Liubov*)   What was it like in Paris? Eh? Did you eat frogs?

LIUBOV   I ate crocodiles.

PISHCHIK   Fancy that!

LOPAKHIN   The days when the countryside was only for landowners and peasants are over. Now it's the time of the summer folk and the weekend visitor. There are dachas around every town, even the smallest, and over the next twenty years or so the summer population is going to explode. So far all they do is sit on their porches and drink tea, but, who knows, they may start using their little acres to grow things and then your cherry orchard will come into its second flowering and be gay and fruitful again . . .

GAEV (*indignantly*)   What is this rubbish?

Varya and Yasha enter.

VARYA   There were two telegrams for you, Mama.

She selects a key and unlocks the book cupboard.

VARYA (*cont.*)   Here.

LIUBOV   They're from Paris.

She tears up the telegrams without reading them.

LIUBOV (*cont.*)   I'm done with Paris.

GAEV   Liuba, do you know how old this book cupboard is? I pulled out the bottom drawer last week and saw there was a date burned into it. This book cupboard was made exactly a hundred years ago. What do you think of that, eh? We might celebrate its centenary. It's an inanimate object but look at it another way, it's, well, it's a book cupboard.

PISHCHIK (*amazed*)   A hundred years! Fancy that!

GAEV   Yes . . . Quite something! . . . (*feeling the book cupboard all over*) Dear old book cupboard! Dear, deeply respected book cupboard, I salute you! For a whole century you have devoted your existence to the highest ideals of truth and goodness—your mute appeal to the creative spirit has never faltered during all your hundred years, (*on the brink of tears*) sustaining our courage and faith in a better future through generations of our blood, and inspiring us to a social conscience for the common good.

Pause.

LOPAKHIN   Quite.

LIUBOV   And you haven't changed either, dear old Lyonya.

GAEV (*somewhat embarrassed*)   In-off into the bottom-right corner and screw back for the middle pocket!

LOPAKHIN (*glancing at his watch*)   I have to get going.

YASHA (*handing Liubov a pill bottle*)   Perhaps you'd like to take your pills now . . . ?

PISHCHIK   You don't need pills, dear lady, they don't do any good, or harm either—give them here, madam . . .

Pishchik takes the pills, pours them into his palm, blows on them, puts them in his mouth and drinks them down with kvass.

PISHCHIK (*cont.*)   There!

LIUBOV (*alarmed*)   You're mad!

PISHCHIK   All gone, swallowed the lot.

LOPAKHIN   Greedy pig!

Everyone laughs.

FIRS When the gentleman was here in Holy Week he got through half a tub of pickled cucumbers . . . (*mutters*)

LIUBOV What is he going on about?

VARYA He's been muttering away like that for years, we've got used to it.

YASHA Ah, the wisdom of old age.

Charlotta Ivanovna in a white dress, very thin, tightly laced, with a lorgnette hanging on her belt, crosses the stage.

LOPAKHIN Forgive me, Charlotta, I haven't had a chance to say hello to you.

Lopakhin tries to kiss her hand.

CHARLOTTA (*pulling it back*) If I let you kiss my hand, it'll be my elbow next and then my shoulder.

LOPAKHIN I'm out of luck today.

Everyone laughs.

LOPAKHIN (*cont.*) Show us a magic trick.

CHARLOTTA Not now. I need my sleep.

She goes out.

LOPAKHIN Well, I'll see you all again in three weeks. (*kissing Liubov's hand*) Goodbye for now—time to go. (*to Gaev*) Goodbye. (*exchanging kisses with Pishchik*) Goodbye. (*giving his hand to Varya, then Firs, and Yasha*) I wish I didn't have to leave. (*to Liubov*) Think it over about the dachas and decide. Let me know, I can get you fifty thousand up front—seriously, think about it.

VARYA (*angrily*) Oh, go if you're going!

LOPAKHIN I'm off—I'm off—

Lopakhin leaves.

GAEV Vulgarian. Oh—sorry!—he's Varya's intended, he's her nice young man.

VARYA Don't say that, uncle.

LIUBOV Oh, come along, Varya—nothing would make me happier. He's a good man.

PISHCHIK A decent fellow, truth be told, one of the most . . . as my Dashenka is the first to say . . . well, she says a lot of things. (*gives a snore, then immediately wakes up again*) Be that as it may, dear lady, if you could lend me two hundred and forty roubles . . . I've got to pay the interest on my mortgage tomorrow . . .

VARYA (*alarmed*) We haven't got it! We haven't!

LIUBOV Honestly, I have nothing.

PISHCHIK Well, it'll turn up from somewhere. (*laughs*) I never lose hope. Just when I'm thinking here we go, all is lost, lo and behold, they build a railway over my land and the money comes in. It will come right again, you'll see— something will turn up, if not today, tomorrow. Dashenka will win the lottery, that ticket's worth two hundred thousand.

LIUBOV Well, I've had my coffee—so it's time for bed.

FIRS (*scolding Gaev*) You've put on your wrong trousers again. What's to be done with you?

VARYA Anya's asleep.

She quietly opens the window. Gaev opens the other window. There is a blaze of white blossom.

VARYA (*cont.*)   The sun's up, it's not cold at all now. Come and see, Mama, look at the orchard, isn't it beautiful? Oh God, breathe the air! And the starlings are singing.

GAEV   The orchard is all in white. Do you remember it, Liuba?—the long avenue as far as you can see, straight as a ribbon, do you remember how it shines on moonlit nights? You haven't forgotten?

LIUBOV (*looking out of the window at the orchard*)   Oh, it's my childhood come back!—innocent days!—when I slept in the nursery and woke with happiness every morning and looked out at the garden. It was just the same, nothing has changed. (*laughs with joy*) White everywhere . . . my orchard!—young again after the gloomy darkness of autumn and the winter cold, and happy again, the angels in heaven haven't forsaken you! Oh, if only I could lose the weight of this stone I carry in my breast. If only I could forget everything up to now!

GAEV   And now the orchard is going to be sold to pay our debts, hard to believe.

LIUBOV   Look!—there's our darling Mama, dressed in white, walking in the orchard! (*laughs with joy*)

GAEV   Where?

VARYA   Bless you, Mama.

LIUBOV   She's gone now. It only looked like it for a minute. There, look, on the right, by the turning toward the summerhouse, that branch bending over like a woman in a white dress.

Enter TROFIMOV. *He wears a worn-out student's uniform and spectacles.*

LIUBOV (*cont.*)   Our orchard is simply the most amazing sight—that mass of white blossom against the blue of the sky . . .

TROFIMOV   Liubov Andreevna!

Liubov looks round at Trofimov.

TROFIMOV (*cont.*)   I only want to pay my respects and then I'll go at once. (*warmly kissing her hand*) They told me to wait till morning but I was too impatient.

Liubov looks at him in bewilderment.

VARYA (*on the brink of tears*)   It's Petya Trofimov, Mama.

TROFIMOV   . . . Yes, your son's old tutor. Have I really changed so much?

Liubov embraces him and softly weeps.

GAEV (*embarrassed*)   There, there, Liuba.

VARYA (*weeps*)   Oh, really, Petya—I said wait till tomorrow.

LIUBOV   My Grisha . . . my little boy . . . Grisha . . . my son . . .

VARYA   What can we do, Mama? It was God's will.

TROFIMOV (*tenderly, on the brink of tears*)   There now . . . there now . . .

LIUBOV (*weeping quietly*)   My little boy died, drowned. (*cries out*) Why? Tell me why, Petya. (*quieter again*) Anya's asleep next door and here I am, raising my voice and making a scene. Let me look at you, Petya. Why have you lost your looks? How did you get so old?

TROFIMOV An old woman on the train yesterday called me "that mangy gentleman."

LIUBOV You were only a boy, a nice young student. Now you're losing your hair and wearing glasses. Are you really still a student?

She goes to the door.

TROFIMOV I expect I'll die a student.

Liubov kisses her brother, then Varya.

LIUBOV Well, now, it's bed time. You've aged too, Leonid.

PISHCHIK (*following her*) Yes, time to get some sleep. Ouch, my gout. I'll stay with you tonight. And in the morning, dearest heart, see your way . . . two hundred and forty roubles . . . ?

GAEV He doesn't give up.

PISHCHIK Two hundred and forty roubles to pay the interest . . . ?

LIUBOV I have no money, my sweet.

PISHCHIK I'll give it back, my dear. It's a trifling sum.

LIUBOV Oh, all right—ask Leonid for it—go on, Leonid—give it to him.

GAEV I give it to him?—he'll be lucky.

LIUBOV What else can one do? He has to have it. He'll pay it back.

Liubov, Trofimov, Pishchik, and Firs go out. Gaev, Varya, and Yasha remain.

GAEV My sister's still in the habit of throwing her money away. (*to Yasha*) Could you stand further away, you smell like a hen house.

YASHA (*with a smirk*) You haven't changed a bit either.

GAEV What? What did he say?

VARYA (*to Yasha*) Your mother's come from the village, she's been sitting in the back hall since yesterday wanting to see you.

YASHA I wish her luck.

VARYA You're shameless.

YASHA What's the rush? Tomorrow would have done.

Yasha goes out.

VARYA Mama's just the same, she hasn't changed at all. Left to herself she'd give away everything she had.

GAEV Yes. (p*ause*) Whenever you have a lot of different remedies prescribed for some disease, it means there's no cure. I've been cudgelling my brains, I can think of lots of remedies, which means, in effect, I haven't got any. If only someone left us lots of money, if only Anya married a millionaire, or we could go to Yaroslavl and try our luck with the countess. Auntie is really enormously rich, you know.

VARYA (*weeps*) If only God would come to our help.

GAEV Don't howl. Auntie's rich but she doesn't like us. To start with, my sister married a lawyer instead of marrying into the nobility . . .

Anya appears in the doorway.

GAEV (*cont.*) ... and having not married into the nobility, she's behaved, well, you couldn't exactly say she's behaved with decorum. She's good and kind, a wonderful woman, and I'm very fond of her, but after making every allowance one can think of, one has to admit she is a woman of loose morals. You only have to look at the way she moves.

VARYA (*whispers*) Anya's there.

GAEV Eh?—what? (*pause*) How odd, I've got something in my eye—I can't see properly. And last Thursday, when I was at the District Court ...

Anya comes forward.

VARYA Why are you still awake, Anya?

ANYA I just can't get to sleep.

GAEV My precious. (*kissing Anya's face and hands*) My little one ... (*on the brink of tears*) you're more my angel than my niece, you're everything to me. It's the truth, believe me.

ANYA I do believe you, uncle. Everyone loves you and looks up to you, but, dear uncle, you must keep quiet, just keep quiet. What were you saying about my mother? About your own sister? What did you have to say that for?

GAEV I know, I know ... (*covering his face with her hand*) That was dreadful of me. Oh God—help me! And I made a speech to a cupboard, how ridiculous—it wasn't till I'd finished that I realised how absurd it was.

VARYA It's true, uncle dear, you should keep quiet, just keep quiet, that's all.

ANYA If you keep quiet you won't go upsetting yourself.

GAEV I'm quiet. (*kisses Anya's and Varya's hands*) Quiet. There's just one thing—it's business. When I was down at the courts on Thursday, well, there was a group of us talking of this and that, and it seems that it might be possible to arrange a loan against a promissory note, enough to pay the bank interest.

VARYA Oh, please God!

GAEV I'll go down there on Tuesday and have another chat. (*to Varya*) Don't howl. (*to Anya*) Your Mama will have a talk with Lopakhin. He'll never refuse her. And when you feel rested, you'll go to Yaroslavl to your great-aunt the countess. So there you are, we'll attack on three fronts and it's in the bag. We'll pay the interest, no doubt about it. (*putting a lemon drop in his mouth*) On my honour—I'll take any oath you like on it, the estate will not be sold!— (*excited*) on my happiness I swear it!—my hand on it, you can call me a worthless cad if the auction goes ahead—I swear it with every particle of my being!

ANYA (*calm and happy again*) You're so good uncle, and so clever. (*embracing her uncle*) I feel calmer now! I'm quite calm! I'm happy!

Firs enters.

FIRS (*reproachfully*) Leonid Andreevich—aren't you ashamed of yourself?—when are you going to bed?

GAEV I'm coming right this minute. You go off, Firs. I'll undress myself. Night-night, my children—we'll settle the details tomorrow, but now time for bed. (*kissing Anya and Varya*) I'm a man of the eighties. That was a period people don't think much of nowadays, but I can say I've suffered for my convictions in my time. It's not for no reason that

I'm loved by the peasant people—one has to know the peasant!—one has to know with whom you're—

ANYA You're doing it, uncle!

VARYA Just be quiet, uncle dear, be quiet.

FIRS (*angrily*) Leonid Andreevich!

GAEV I'm going, I'm going. Off to bed. Cushion, cushion, and into the middle pocket!—pot white!

Gaev goes out, Firs shuffles after him.

ANYA (*as they go*) Thank you, uncle. I'm easier in my mind now. I don't fancy going to my great-aunt's, I don't like her . . . but I do feel better.

Anya sits down.

VARYA You must go to sleep. I'm going to. Something really upsetting happened while you were away. You know the old servants' quarters—nobody lives there now except a few of the ancients—Yefimyushka, Polya, Yevstignei, oh, and Karp, too. Well, they started letting stray people stay the night, suspicious characters passing through. I said nothing about it. Only, then I hear they're putting it about I'd given orders that they're fed on nothing but dried peas. Out of meanness, if you please, and Yevstignei's behind it. Right, I thought—if that's the case, just you wait. I send for him. (*yawns*) He comes in. What's this you've been saying about me, you old fool? (*glancing at Anya*) Anechka! . . . (*pause*) Fallen asleep . . .

Varya takes Anya by the arm.

VARYA (*cont.*) Let's be off to bed . . . come along! . . . (*leading her*) My little sleepyhead! Come along . . .

Varya and Anya move off.

In the distance, beyond the orchard, a shepherd plays a pipe. Trofimov enters and, seeing Varya and Anya, stops.

VARYA (*cont.*)   Shhh . . . sleepy time . . . come along, darling . . .

ANYA (*softly, half asleep*)   I'm so tired . . . I can still hear the harness bells . . . uncle . . . dear uncle, and Mama too . . .

VARYA   Here we go, my lamb . . . this way . . .

They go into Anya's room.

TROFIMOV (*moved*)   My little ray of sunshine! My springtime!

CURTAIN

ACT TWO

Outdoors among open fields: an old, long-abandoned, leaning little chapel; alongside it a well, large stones, which appear to be old gravestones, and an old bench. The track leading to the Gaevs' estate can be seen. To one side, rise up the dark shapes of poplars where the cherry orchard begins. In the distance there is a row of telegraph poles, and beyond, on the horizon, a large town can just be made out, visible only on clear days. The sun will soon be setting.

Charlotta, Yasha and Dunyasha are sitting on the bench, lost in thought, while YEPIKHODOV stands beside them, playing something sad on a guitar. Charlotta, wearing an old cap, has taken a gun from her shoulder and is adjusting the buckle on the strap.

CHARLOTTA (*meditatively*)   I've never had any proper papers, I don't know how old I am, and I always think of myself as young. When I was little my father and Mama used to go round the fairs doing their shows, very good shows they were, too. And I'd do the leap of death and other tricks. Then when papa and Mama died, a German lady took me in and started giving me lessons. Well and good, so I grew up and went to be a governess. But who I am and where I'm from, I really don't know, or who my parents were or whether perhaps they weren't married, I don't know. (*takes a cucumber from her pocket and eats it*) I don't know anything. I long to have someone to talk to, but there isn't anybody. I don't have anyone.

YEPIKHODOV (*plays the guitar and sings*)   "What do I care for the noisy world? Friend or foe, I hear you not . . ."

It's a lovely thing to play the mandolin!

DUNYASHA   It's not a mandolin, it's a guitar.

29

Dunyasha looks in a small hand-mirror and powders herself.

YEPIKHODOV For us who are mad for love it's a mandolin . . . (*starts to sing and Yasha joins in*) "If only the girl I gave my heart would give her heart to me . . ."

CHARLOTTA What a horrible noise. They sing like hyenas, these people.

DUNYASHA (*to Yasha*) Still, you're so lucky to have been abroad.

YASHA Yes, I have to agree.

Yasha yawns, then lights a cigar.

YEPIKHODOV Naturally. Abroad has been going on for ages, it's arrived at a certain state of arrival.

YASHA Stands to reason.

YEPIKHODOV I'm someone who keeps up, I've read all sorts of amazing books, and yet I can't work out the tendency of my inclination, to be or to shoot myself, that is the question. So I always carry a revolver to be on the safe side, look. (*shows the revolver*)

CHARLOTTA Done. I'm off. (*slinging the rifle over her shoulder*) Yepikhodov, you're a brilliant fellow and very scary. Women should be throwing themselves at you. Grrr! (*as she goes*) I'm surrounded by brainy idiots. There's no one I can talk to, I'm all alone, utterly alone, I have no one, and who I am and what I'm doing here is a mystery.

Charlotta goes out, unhurriedly.

YEPIKHODOV Speaking for myself, I'll say one thing about me apart from anything else, which is that fate has got it in for me like a big storm for a small boat. If I'm wrong, supposing, why is it, for instance, that when I woke up this morning there was an enormous spider sitting on my chest? As big as this. (*indicating with both his hands*) Another example. I have a drink and there at the bottom of my glass is something utterly revolting, a cockroach or something. (*pause*) Have you read Buckle's *History of Civilisation in England*? (*pause*) Dunyasha, could I trouble you for a couple of words?

DUNYASHA Go ahead.

YEPIKHODOV I'd prefer to have them in private.

Yepikhodov sighs, Dunyasha is embarrassed.

DUNYASHA Oh, all right . . . but first could you bring my cape from indoors beside the cupboard . . . I'm feeling the damp out here.

YEPIKHODOV Yes, all right. I'll go and fetch it. Now I know what to do with my revolver . . .

Yepikhodov takes the guitar and begins to play as he goes out.

YASHA Poor old Catastrophe! Entre nous, the man's a moron. (*yawns*)

DUNYASHA God, I hope he's not going to shoot himself. (*pause*) Everything makes me nervous, I'm so anxious all the time. Master and Mistress took me in when I was a little girl, and I've got unused to simple ways. Look at my hands, they're white like a lady's hands. I've become so sensitive I'm frightened of everything, it's awful. If you deceive me, Yasha, I don't know if my nerves could stand it.

YASHA (*kissing her*) My little cabbage! Of course, a girl must know her place. If there's one thing I can't stand it's a girl who doesn't know how to behave herself.

DUNYASHA I'm terribly in love with you. You're educated. You know what to think about everything. (*pause*)

YASHA (*yawns*) True, true. To my way of thinking, if a girl falls in love, she's asking for it. (*pause*) There's nothing like a cigar in the fresh air . . . (*listens*) They're coming this way, it's the Mistress and that lot.

Dunyasha kisses him impulsively.

YASHA (*cont.*) Go back to the house—take the path from the river as though you've been for a swim, otherwise you'll meet them and they'll think I'm keeping company with you—I can't be doing with that.

DUNYASHA (*quietly coughing*) Your cigar's given me a headache.

Dunyasha goes out.

Yasha puts out his cigar and remains, sitting beside the chapel. Liubov Andreevna, Gaev, and Lopakhin enter.

LOPAKHIN You have to decide once and for all. Time will not wait for you. The question couldn't be simpler. Will you agree to give the land over to building plots, or not? Yes or no?

LIUBOV Who's been smoking cheap cigars?

Liubov sits down.

GAEV It's so convenient now they've built the railway— lunch in town and home again. (*sitting down*) Pot red into the middle pocket. I wouldn't mind going up to the house for a game now . . .

LIUBOV You'll have plenty of time.

LOPAKHIN Just say one word! (*pleading*) Give me an answer!

GAEV (*yawning*)   To what?

LIUBOV (*looking in her purse*)   There was lots of money in here yesterday, and now there's hardly any. Poor Varya's economising, feeding us on slops, and the old ones in the kitchen only get dried peas . . . and here am I spending money without a thought, I don't know where it goes . . . (*the purse drops, scattering coins*) And now I've dropped it everywhere . . .

Liubov is annoyed. Yasha gathers the coins.

YASHA   Allow me, I'll pick it up.

LIUBOV   Be so kind, Yasha. And why ever did I go out for lunch? That frightful restaurant of yours, with that music and tablecloths smelling of soap . . . Why do you drink so much, Lyonya? And eat so much? Why do you talk so much? In the restaurant you were rambling on about the seventies and the Decadents, and for whose benefit? Who but you would lecture the waiters about the Decadent movement?

LOPAKHIN   No one.

GAEV (*making a dismissive gesture*)   Clearly I'm beyond help. (*irritably, to Yasha*) Why are you always hovering about in front of my face?

YASHA (*laughs*)   Just hearing your voice makes me laugh.

GAEV (*to his sister*)   It's him or me.

LIUBOV   Go away, Yasha, go on.

YASHA (*handing Liubov her purse*)   I'm going. (*barely restraining his laughter*) I've gone.

Yasha goes out.

LOPAKHIN   That millionaire Deriganov wants to buy your estate. They say he's coming to the auction in person.

LIUBOV   Who told you?

LOPAKHIN   It's what they're saying in town.

GAEV   Our aunt in Yaroslavl has promised to let us have some money, we don't know how much . . .

LOPAKHIN   A hundred thousand? Two hundred thousand?

LIUBOV   Oh, really! Ten, perhaps fifteen thousand, and lucky to get that.

LOPAKHIN   Forgive me for saying so, but you two are the most irresponsible, the strangest, most unbusinesslike people I've ever met. I'm telling you in words of one syllable that your house and land are about to be sold off, and it just doesn't get through.

LIUBOV   Well, what are we supposed to do about it? Go on, tell us.

LOPAKHIN   I tell you every day. I keep telling you. You have to lease out the cherry orchard and your land for summer cottages—right now—as soon as you can. The auction is coming and soon. Get that into your heads! The moment you give the word, you'll get all the money you want, and you'll be saved.

LIUBOV   Summer cottages and weekenders . . . I'm sorry but it's all so tawdry.

GAEV   Couldn't agree more.

LOPAKHIN   I'm going to scream or burst into tears, or faint clean away—I can't do it anymore, you're driving me crazy. (*to Gaev*) You old woman!

GAEV Who?

LOPAKHIN (*going*) You! I said you're an old woman!

LIUBOV (*frightened*) Oh—don't go away, please don't go, my dear. Perhaps we'll think of something!

LOPAKHIN What more is there to think about!

LIUBOV Please, please stay! You cheer me up somehow, despite yourself. (*pause*) I keep expecting something to happen, as though the house were to fall around our ears.

GAEV (*deep in thought*) Screw back off the cushion into the corner pocket—cross over for the middle pocket . . .

LIUBOV We must be paying for our sins . . . so many sins . . .

LOPAKHIN Oh, yes? And what sins would they be?

GAEV (*putting a sweet in his mouth*) They say I've consumed my patrimony in lemon drops . . . (*laughs*)

LIUBOV Oh, my sins! I've always squandered money without a thought like some madwoman, and then I married a man who did nothing but run up debts. My husband died of champagne, he was a terrible drinker. Then I had the misfortune to fall in love and take up with someone else just at the moment when . . . and this was my first punishment, like a blow to the head—it was here—here in this river, my little boy drowned, and I went abroad, I didn't pause—I meant never to return, to see this river ever again. I shut my eyes and fled, not knowing where I was going, and he came after me, he wouldn't give up, he was merciless. I bought a little house near Menton when he fell ill there, and for the next three years I had no rest day or night, he wore me out, my soul dried up. Then last year when the house had to go to pay the debts, I went to Paris, and there he robbed me of everything. He threw me over and went off with another woman, and I tried to poison myself. It was all so stupid and humiliating. And all of a sudden I knew I had to come back to Russia, to my home, to my daughter. (*wipes away tears*) Oh God forgive me, forgive my sins! Don't punish me any more! (*takes a telegram from her pocket*). I got this from Paris this morning. He asks me to forgive him, and implores me to go back. (*tears up the telegram*) Isn't that music I can hear? (*listens*)

GAEV   That's our famous Jewish orchestra. Do you remember them? Four fiddles with flute and double bass.

LIUBOV   Are they still going? We must have them up to the house some time, arrange an evening.

LOPAKHIN (*listening*)   I can't hear anything. (*softly sings*) "Russians is what we are, we pay the Germans to make us French . . ." I went to the theatre last night, saw a very funny play . . .

LIUBOV   I bet it wasn't. People shouldn't go to plays, they should spend the time looking in the mirror, at their grey lives and pointless conversations.

LOPAKHIN   You're right. The truth is life is a stupid business. (*pause*) My father was a typical peasant, a fool who knew nothing. Taught me nothing, just beat me with his stick when he got drunk. In actual fact I'm not much different, an ignoramus and a clod. I've no education, my handwriting is so bad I'm ashamed for people to see it, it's like if a pig could write.

LIUBOV   What you need to do, my dear, is get married.

LOPAKHIN   Yes . . . true enough.

LIUBOV To someone like our Varya. She's a good girl.

LOPAKHIN She is.

LIUBOV She comes from simple folk, so she can work all day long, but the main thing is she's in love with you. And you've liked her for a long time, haven't you?

LOPAKHIN Well, yes. I'm not against it. She's a good girl.

Pause.

GAEV They're offering me a place in the bank. Six thousand a year. Had you heard?

LIUBOV What, you in a bank? You just stay where you are. Sit tight.

Firs enters; he has brought an overcoat.

FIRS (*to Gaev*) Please be so good, sir, put this on or you'll get damp.

GAEV (*putting on the overcoat*) You're a damn nuisance, dear friend.

FIRS Sticks and stones. You didn't tell me you were going out.

Firs looks Gaev over.

LIUBOV You've got so old, Firs!

FIRS What can I do for you?

LOPAKHIN She says you've got old!

FIRS Well, I've lived a long time. I was being married off before your father had even come into this world. (*laughs*) And when the freedom was declared I was already head valet. I didn't take my freedom. I stayed with Master and

Mistress. (*pause*) I remember how everyone was happy, little did they know.

LOPAKHIN   Oh yes, they were good times before '61, you could be flogged in those days.

FIRS (*mishearing*)   I should say so! The peasants belonged to the masters and the masters belonged to the peasants, but now it's all higgledy-piggledy, you don't know *where* you are.

GAEV   That's enough from you for now, Firs. I'm going into town tomorrow. I've been promised an introduction to a general who might put up some money against my signature.

LOPAKHIN   It'll come to nothing, and anyway what would you pay the interest with?

LIUBOV   He's raving. There aren't any generals.

Trofimov, Anya, and Varya are seen.

GAEV   Ah, here are some more of us.

ANYA   Mama's over there, look.

LIUBOV (*tenderly*)   Come and join us. Come over, my darlings. (*embracing Anya and Varya*) You don't know how much I love you both, come and sit by me.

Everyone sits down.

LOPAKHIN   The Eternal Student's never far from the young ladies.

TROFIMOV   What's that to you?

LOPAKHIN   He's coming up to his pension and he's still a student.

TROFIMOV   We can do without your inane jokes.

LOPAKHIN   What's the matter, you funny chap—are you getting cross?

TROFIMOV   Just stop going on at me.

LOPAKHIN (*laughs*)   Well, answer me one thing. What do you think about me?

TROFIMOV   I think you're necessary. You're a rich man and getting richer. The cycle of nature requires carnivores to eat whatever comes their way. It's called the conversion of matter.

Everyone laughs.

VARYA   Petya, tell us about the planets, they're safer ground.

LIUBOV   No, let's go on where we left off yesterday.

TROFIMOV   What was that?

GAEV   Human pride.

TROFIMOV   Oh, yes. We talked for ages yesterday about how we pride ourselves on being human, but we didn't get anywhere. In your mind there's something mystical in our idea of ourselves, and maybe it's true for you, but if we take the simplest view of things, what have we got to be so proud of when man as a physiological machine is so inefficient? I mean, what sense does it make when the vast majority of us are brutish, ignorant, and profoundly unhappy? We have to stop admiring ourselves. Only work can save us.

GAEV   You're just as dead in the end.

TROFIMOV Who knows? What does it mean—to be dead? Maybe we have a hundred senses and it's only the five we know that die, and the other ninety-five continue on.

LIUBOV You're so clever, Petya!

LOPAKHIN (*ironically*) Brilliant!

TROFIMOV Mankind is advancing, developing its powers. Everything which is as yet out of reach is coming closer to our grasp and our understanding, but we have to work, work with all our might, to support those who are seeking the truth of things. In Russia so far, very few of us are working. With few exceptions, the intelligentsia, from what I've seen of them, seek nothing, do nothing, they don't want to work and wouldn't know how. They call themselves the intelligentsia but they treat their servants like children, and peasants like animals, they don't know how to study, don't read anything serious, they may as well not bother— science is only there to chatter about, and needless to say they don't know much about art. They're all so earnest, with such serious faces, talking and philosophising away about deep important things, and all the while in front of their eyes, the masses are fed on filth, no pillows to their beds, thirty or forty to a room, and everywhere bedbugs, stench, damp, and moral degradation. It's obvious that all the fine talk is just to distract attention, theirs and ours. Perhaps you can tell me, where are all those nursery schools everyone talks about? Where are those reading rooms? You only see them in novels, they don't actually exist. There's nothing out there but dirt, banality, and backwardness. I'm afraid of those serious faces and their serious conversations. It's better to say nothing at all.

LOPAKHIN Well, let me tell you—I'm up every day before five o'clock. I work from morning till night, and yes, I'm constantly handling money, mine and other people's, and I get a good look at what people around me are like. You only have to try to get something done and you soon find out how few decent, reliable people there are. Sometimes when I can't sleep, I think, "Dear Lord, you have given us these vast forests and boundless plains to the wide horizon— living here we should really be giants!"

LIUBOV   How would it help being giants? Giants are all very well in fairy tales but anywhere else they'd just frighten everybody.

Behind them, Yepikhodov crosses and quietly, mournfully playing his guitar.

LIUBOV (*cont.*) (*pensively*)   There goes Yepikhodov . . .

ANYA (*echoing*)   There goes Yepikhodov . . .

GAEV   Well, ladies and gentlemen, the sun's gone down.

TROFIMOV   Yes.

GAEV (*softly, as if reciting*)   Oh, wondrous nature, glowing with an eternal fire, so beautiful and so indifferent, you whom we call mother, life and death are united in you, you give life and you destroy it.

VARYA (*imploringly*)   Uncle!

ANYA   You're doing it, uncle!

TROFIMOV   You'd better stick to potting red off the cushion.

GAEV   I am silent. Silent.

They all sit lost in thought. Silence. All that can be heard is Firs muttering quietly. Suddenly a distant sound breaks the silence, as though from the sky: the sound of a breaking string, dying away, a sense of melancholy.

LIUBOV What was that?

LOPAKHIN I don't know. A cable broke somewhere way off, in the mines but far, far away.

GAEV It could have been some kind of bird . . . something like a heron.

TROFIMOV Or an owl.

LIUBOV (*shudders*) There was something sinister about it, I don't know why . . .

FIRS It was just the same before the disaster. The owl shrieked and the samovar wouldn't stop moaning.

GAEV Before what disaster?

FIRS The Freedom.

Pause.

LIUBOV Well, I say we should go in, the evening's upon us. (*to Anya*) You've got tears in your eyes . . . what is it, my darling?

She embraces Anya.

ANYA It's nothing, Mama, I'm all right.

TROFIMOV Someone's coming.

A PASSER-BY enters. He wears an overcoat and a tattered peaked cap. He is tipsy.

PASSER-BY Excuse me, can I get to the station through here?

GAEV You can. Follow the track.

PASSER-BY Much obliged. (*with a cough*) What wonderful weather . . . (*recites*) "To the Volga! The sounds that call us to Russia's great river belong to the groans and cries of the haulers! Pity the land that calls it a song!" (*to Varya*) Mademoiselle, spare thirty kopecks for a hungry fellow-countryman.

Varya takes fright, and shrieks.

LOPAKHIN (*angrily*)   Hey, you!—watch your step!

LIUBOV (*panicky*)   Here take this. . . . (*searching in her purse*) I have no silver—never mind, here's ten roubles.

PASSER-BY   Deeply grateful to you!

The Passer-by goes on his way and the others laugh.

VARYA (*frightened*)   I'm going in. Honestly, Mama, we can't feed the servants and you gave him a gold piece.

LIUBOV   I know, I'm such a fool. What's to be done with me? I'll give you all I've got left when we get home. Yermolai Alekseevich, you'll lend me some more won't you?

LOPAKHIN   Your humble servant.

LIUBOV   Come along, everyone. Oh, and by the way, Varya, we got you engaged to be married, congratulations.

VARYA (*on the brink of tears*)   It's nothing to make jokes about.

LOPAKHIN   Get thee to a scullery.

GAEV   My hands are shaking. It's a long time since I had a game of billiards.

LOPAKHIN   Nymph, in thy orisons, be all your sinks remembered.

LIUBOV   Off we go. It's nearly time for supper.

VARYA   That man frightened me. My heart's still thumping.

LOPAKHIN A final reminder, ladies and gentlemen: on August 22nd the cherry orchard will be sold. So think on that! Keep thinking!

They all go out, except Trofimov and Anya.

ANYA (*laughing*) We should thank that man for scaring Varya. Now there's no one but us.

TROFIMOV Varya's afraid we'll fall in love, that's why she follows us about day after day. Her narrow mind can't grasp that we're above and beyond what she calls love. The goal and meaning of our life is to reject all the banal illusions that keep us from being happy and free. Onward! On to that bright star burning ahead of us in the far distance! Nothing can stop us! Don't fall behind, my comrades!

ANYA (*clasping her hands with emotion*) How beautifully you say things! (*pause*) It's been a wonderful day.

TROFIMOV Yes—what weather.

ANYA What have you done to me, Petya? Why have I stopped feeling the way I used to about the cherry orchard? I loved it so dearly, I thought there was no lovelier place on God's earth.

TROFIMOV The whole of Russia is our orchard. The world is vast and there are many lovely places in it. (*pause*) Just think, Anya—your grandfather, and his father, and all your family going back, they owned living souls. The dead are looking at you and whispering to you from every tree in the cherry orchard, from every leaf and every branch. The ownership of human beings! You're all of you corrupted by it, Anya, don't you see?—the present generation no less, so corrupted neither you, your mother, your uncle, notice any more that you owe your life to people you wouldn't even let in your front door. This country is two hundred years behind and falling back, because we haven't come to terms with our history, we just philosophise on, or complain we're bored, or get drunk. But it's so clear that to live in the present we have to redeem our past, finish with it, and it's going to hurt, there's no easy way—we have to work till we drop. You must see that, Anya.

ANYA Our house isn't ours, it hasn't been ours for a long time. I'll leave it behind me—I promise you, Petya.

TROFIMOV Throw the keys down the well and go. Free as the wind.

ANYA (*in delight*) Free as the wind! That's beautiful!

TROFIMOV Believe in me, Anya—believe in me! I'm not yet thirty, I'm young, I'm still a student, but I know about suffering. In winter time I've been hungry, ill, anxious, poor as a beggar—every corner fate can drive a man to, I've been there. And still, the whole time, every second of the day and night, my soul has been filled with a sense of things to come, an inexpressible, indescribable feeling of happiness to come—I can see it now, Anya.

ANYA (*pensively*) The moon is rising.

Yepikhodov can be heard playing the same sad song on the guitar. The moon rises. Somewhere, near the poplars, Varya is looking for Anya.

VARYA'S VOICE Anya! Where are you?

TROFIMOV Yes, the moon is rising. (*pause*) There it is— happiness, here it comes, nearer and nearer—I can hear its footsteps . . . and if we don't live to see it, and never know it for ourselves, what does it matter? There's others who will!

45

VARYA'S VOICE Anya! Where are you?

TROFIMOV It's Varya again! (*angrily*) She's such a pain!

ANYA Come on, let's go down to the river. It's nice there.

TROFIMOV Yes, come on, then.

Anya and Trofimov move off.

VARYA'S VOICE Anya! Anya!

CURTAIN

ACT THREE

The drawing room, with an arch leading to the ballroom. The chandelier is lit. The Jewish orchestra, the same one that has been mentioned in the second act, can be heard playing in the entrance hall. Evening. In the ballroom they are dancing the grand rond. The voice of Simeonov-Pishchik: 'Promenade à une paire!' Couples dance through the drawing room: Pishchik and Charlotta Ivanovna, Trofimov and Liubov Andreevna, Anya and the POST OFFICE CLERK, Varya and the STATION MASTER, and others. Varya is crying quietly, wiping away tears as she dances. In the final pair is Dunyasha. They circle the drawing room, and dance out.

PISHCHIK *(calls out)*   Grand rond, balancez! Les cavaliers à genoux et remerciez vos dames!

Firs, in tails, brings seltzer water on a tray. Pishchik and Trofimov come into the drawing room.

PISHCHIK *(cont.)*   High blood pressure. I've already had a couple of scares. Dancing is a strain for me, but as they say, if you run with the pack—them as don't bark, wag your tails! I'm strong as a horse really. My dear late father, may he rest in peace, used to joke the Simeonov-Pishchiks were descended from Caligula's horse, the one he made consul. *(sitting down)* But my problem is I've got no money. A hungry dog can't think of anything but meat . . . *(snores, and then straight away wakes up)* And it's the same with me and money.

TROFIMOV   Come to think of it, there's something horsey about your hindquarters.

PISHCHIK   Well, nothing wrong with that. A horse is all right. You can get a price for a horse.

47

People can be heard playing billiards in the next room. Varya appears in the archway into the ballroom.

TROFIMOV (*teasing*) It's Madame Lopakhina!

VARYA (*snaps*) Mangy young gentleman!

TROFIMOV Mangy and proud of it!

VARYA (*bitterly*) So we've gone and hired a band, and how are we supposed to pay for it?

Varya goes out.

TROFIMOV When I think of the effort you've put into chasing money all your life, if you'd put that energy to better use you could have changed the world by now.

PISHCHIK Nietzsche, the philosopher, a great and famous man, a man of enormous intellect, says somewhere that it's all right to forge banknotes.

TROFIMOV (*incredulous*) You've *read* Nietzsche?

PISHCHIK Not exactly, but my Dashenka's told me. And at this moment my situation is so desperate, I'd forge a few banknotes myself. The day after tomorrow I have to pay three hundred and ten roubles. I've got together a hundred and thirty. (*feels in his pockets, alarmed*) It's gone! I've lost my money! (*almost bursting into tears*) Where's it gone? (*joyfully*) Oh—it's here, in the lining. I've come out in a cold sweat.

Liubov and Charlotta enter. Liubov is humming a Caucasian dance melody.

LIUBOV What's keeping Leonid? What can he be doing in town? (*to Dunyasha*) See if the musicians want some tea, Dunyasha.

TROFIMOV   The auction was probably cancelled.

LIUBOV   It wasn't the best moment to have a band and throw a party. Well, let's not worry about that.

Liubov sits down and softly hums. Charlotta hands Pishchik a pack of cards.

CHARLOTTA   Think of a card, any card.

PISHCHIK   All right, I've thought of one.

CHARLOTTA   Now shuffle the pack. Very good. Let me have it, mon cher Monsieur Pishchik. Ein, zwei, drei! Is that your card in your side pocket?

PISHCHIK   (*takes a card from out of his pocket*)   Eight of spades, absolutely right! (*amazed*) Fancy that!

Charlotta holds the pack of cards in her palm, to Trofimov.

CHARLOTTA   Top card—don't think—what is it?

TROFIMOV   What card? Well, queen of spades.

CHARLOTTA   (*shows it*)   So it is! (*to Pishchik*) Which one now?

PISHCHIK   Ace of hearts.

CHARLOTTA   (*shows it*)   So it is!

She claps her palms together, and the pack of cards disappears.

CHARLOTTA   (*cont.*)   Well, lovely weather we're having!

A mysterious female voice answers her, as though coming from under the floor.

VOICE   Oh indeed, lovely weather, my dear.

STATION MASTER   Who said that?

CHARLOTTA   You're a woman after my own heart.

VOICE   You're not so bad yourself, my dear.

STATION MASTER (*applauding*)   That was her as well! She's a ventriloquist!

PISHCHIK (*amazed*)   Fancy that! You're an amazing girl, Miss Charlotta—I think I'm in love.

CHARLOTTA   In love? (*shrugging her shoulders*) It takes more than that. You may have the instrument but can you play the music . . . ?

Trofimov claps Pishchik on the shoulder and neighs.

CHARLOTTA (*cont.*)   Your attention, please. For my last trick.

Charlotta takes a throw from a chair.

CHARLOTTA (*cont.*)   I have here a very nice rug for sale.

She shakes the cloth.

CHARLOTTA (*cont.*)   Who would like to buy it?

PISHCHIK   Fancy that . . .

CHARLOTTA   Ein, zwei, drei!

Charlotta sweeps aside the cloth. Anya is standing behind it; she makes a curtsey, runs over to her mother, embraces her, and then runs back into the ballroom amid general delight.

LIUBOV (*applauds*)   Bravo, bravo!

CHARLOTTA   And again! Ein, zwei, drei.

Charlotta sweeps aside the cloth; behind it stands Varya, who bows.

PISHCHIK (*amazed*)   Fancy that!

CHARLOTTA The end!

Charlotta throws the rug at Pishchik, makes a bow and runs out of the ballroom.

PISHCHIK She's a witch! That's what she is! Don't you think?

Pishchik follows her out.

LIUBOV And still no Leonid. What can he be doing in town all this time? Everything must be over by now. Either the estate is sold or the auction didn't happen, so why are we being kept in suspense?

VARYA (*consoling*) Uncle bought it, I know it.

TROFIMOV (*sarcastically*) Oh yes, I'm sure.

VARYA Auntie signed him her authority to buy it for her and transfer the mortgage. She's done it for Anya, and by God's grace uncle will have bought it.

LIUBOV She sent us 15,000 roubles to bid in her name—on our own property, she doesn't even trust us—and the money wouldn't even cover the mortgage. (*covers her face with her hands*) The rest of my life is being decided today, my whole fate is under the hammer.

TROFIMOV (*teasing Varya*) Madame Lopakhina!

VARYA (*angrily*) The Wandering Student! Thrown out of two different universities so far!

LIUBOV What are you getting so cross about, Varya? He's only teasing. And why shouldn't he? Go ahead and marry Lopakhin if you want to, he's a decent, interesting man. And if you don't want to, then don't. Nobody's forcing you, my darling.

VARYA I'm serious about him, Mama, if you want to know. He's a good man, and I do like him.

LIUBOV Then marry him. I don't understand what you're waiting for.

VARYA Well, I can't propose to him, Mama! Everybody's been talking about me marrying him for the last two years, but he never says anything, or he makes jokes. It's not hard to understand. He's busy making money, he doesn't have time for me. If I had any money of my own, even a little, if I had even a hundred roubles, I'd give up everything and go my own way. I'd enter a convent.

TROFIMOV Oh, what a glorious thought!

VARYA (*to Trofimov*) I thought students were supposed to be intelligent. (*quietly, on the brink of tears*) How unattractive you've become, Petya, you look so old. (*to Liubov, no longer crying*) It's just that I can't do with having nothing to do, Mama—I need to be doing something every minute of the day.

Yasha enters, barely containing his laughter.

YASHA Yepikhodov has broken a billiard cue!

Yasha goes out.

VARYA What's he doing here? Who gave him permission to play billiards? These people are beyond me.

Varya goes out.

LIUBOV You shouldn't tease her, Petya. You can see she's unhappy enough as things are.

TROFIMOV She's far too bossy, sticking her nose in everybody else's business. All summer she wouldn't give me and Anya any peace, terrified we might start a romance. What's it got to do with her? Anyway, I've done nothing to put the idea into her head, I'm above all that. Anya and I are far above anything as banal as love.

LIUBOV And I suppose I'm far beneath it. (*greatly agitated*) Why isn't my brother here? If only I knew whether the estate has been sold or not. I just can't believe that such a terrible thing could happen to us, but I can't control myself much longer—I'm ready to scream out loud, do something mad. Help me, Petya, say something.

TROFIMOV What difference does it make whether the estate is sold or not sold? It was all over long ago and you can't go back, the bridges are burned. Calm down, and stop fooling yourself—for once in your life you have to face up to the truth.

LIUBOV Whose truth? You can tell what's true and not true, but I seem to have lost my sight, I can't see anything. You're so sure you've got all the answers. But, my love, isn't that because you're too young to have lived out a single one of your questions? You can look at the future without blinking, and isn't that because you're not expecting to see the terrible things life has still got hidden from your innocent eyes? We're not so brave as you, not so honest, or so intellectual, but spare a thought, show a fingertip of generosity, just enough to take pity on me. After all, I was born here, my parents and grandparents lived and died here, I love this house, I can't make sense of my life without the cherry orchard, and if it has to be sold, sell me with it. (*embracing Trofimov, kissing him on the forehead*) My son drowned here, you know that . . . (*weeping*) You're good and kind, so show some pity.

TROFIMOV   You know you have my sincere sympathy.

LIUBOV   That's not the same thing. (*as she takes out a handkerchief, a telegram drops to the floor*) I feel so desperate today, you can't imagine. Everything's so noisy here, I can't bear it, my heart jumps at every sound, I'm shaking, and I can't go and find somewhere quiet because when I'm by myself I'm frightened by the silence. Don't judge me, Petya —I'm as fond of you as though you were my own child. I'd happily let you marry Anya, truly I would, only, my dearest boy, you must study and get your degree. You don't do anything, you let fate blow you this way and that, it's not normal. That's true, isn't it? And you really must do something about that beard, you must encourage it. (*laughs*) You are a funny-looking boy.

TROFIMOV   (*picks up the telegram*)   I'm not interested in how I look.

LIUBOV   It's a telegram from Paris. I get one every day. One yesterday, another today. That wild man is in a bad way again, he's ill. He asks to be forgiven, begs me to come back, and I really should go to Paris to be near him for a while. Don't look like that, Petya, what else can I do?—he's sick and all on his own, and unhappy—who's going to look after him there, who's going to stop him getting into a pickle again, and make sure he takes his medicine? Why bother to deny it, I love him, that much I know. I love him. Love!—it's the millstone round my neck and I'll go to the bottom with it, but I love love and I won't live without it. (*squeezes Trofimov's hand*) Don't think badly of me, Petya . . . don't say anything.

TROFIMOV   (*on the brink of tears*)   Please . . . please God forgive my bluntness but that man stole everything you had, he robbed you!

LIUBOV (*covering her ears*)   No, no, you mustn't say that.

TROFIMOV   But he's such a swine and everyone knows it except you—he's an insignificant crook, a nobody.

LIUBOV (*irritated, but restrained*)   You are twenty-six or seven, and you talk like a schoolboy in short trousers.

TROFIMOV   Well, what if I do!

LIUBOV   It's about time you were a man, at your age you should understand about love. You still need to find out, you need to fall in love yourself! (*angrily*) Yes, that's what it is!—you're not pure, you're just late! You're nothing but a prude and a prig, a freak—fancy, the age you are and no lover!

TROFIMOV (*in horror*)   What are you saying!

LIUBOV   "Above love"! You're not above love—as Firs would say, you're a noodle. Twenty-six and never been kissed!

TROFIMOV (*in horror*)   This is horrible! What is she talking about?

Trofimov goes quickly into the ballroom, clutching his head.

TROFIMOV (*cont.*)   It's awful—I can't—I'm leaving—

He goes out, but immediately comes back.

TROFIMOV (*cont.*)   It's over between us!

He goes out into the entrance hall.

LIUBOV (*shouting after him*)   Petya, wait! Don't be silly, Petya! I was only joking!

Someone can be heard quickly going up the stairs in the entrance hall and then suddenly falling downstairs with a crash. Anya and Varya shriek, but then straight away laughter can be heard.

LIUBOV (*cont.*)   What's going on?

Anya runs in.

ANYA (*laughing*)   Petya's fallen down the stairs!

Anya runs out.

LIUBOV (*following Anya*)   There's something very odd about that boy.

The Station Master comes and stands in the middle of the ballroom.

STATION MASTER   I would like to give you "The Scarlet Woman" by A. Tolstoy! "The Scarlet Woman."
>There was gaiety and laughter,
>The singing shook the rafter!
>Crystal shattered in the music's din.
>But who is she who sits alone
>And stares like one with a life to atone?
>It's the woman who lived in sin!
>There was revelling and feasting, and the . . .

The strains of a waltz come from the entrance hall. The recitation is broken off by A GUEST who has detected the faux pas, and hustles the protesting, puzzled Station Master away as they all dance. Trofimov, Anya, Varya, and Liubov Andreevna come in from the entrance hall.

LIUBOV   So there you are, Petya—pure-in-heart and above it all!—I'm sorry! Dance with me.

Liubov and Petya dance.

Anya and Varya dance. Firs enters, leans his stick by the side door. Yasha has also come in from the drawing room, and is watching the dancing.

YASHA   So what are you for, granddad?

FIRS I'm not well. In the old days, we used to entertain generals, barons, admirals, and now we invite the clerk from the post office and the station master, and even they have to be dragged along. I've got a bit wobbly somehow. The old master, her grandfather, he used to swear by powdered sealing wax to treat all kinds of ailments. I've been taking sealing wax every day for twenty years or more—it's probably why I'm still alive.

YASHA You're getting on my wick, granddad—(*yawns*) Why don't you die and be done with it?

FIRS Ekh! You . . . noodle.

He continues to mutter. Trofimov and Liubov Andreevna dance from the ballroom into the drawing room.

LIUBOV Merci! I must sit down a minute. (*sitting down*) I'm exhausted.

Anya enters.

ANYA (*agitated*) There was a man in the kitchen saying the cherry orchard was sold today!

LIUBOV Sold? To whom?

ANYA He didn't say. He's gone now.

Trofimov claims her for a dance. They dance out into the ballroom.

YASHA It was just some old tramp gossiping, a stranger.

FIRS And Leonid Andreevich isn't home yet. He took his light overcoat. Before you know it he'll catch a chill. Ekh! Young in years, end in tears.

LIUBOV I'm going to drop down dead in a minute. Yasha, go and find out who bought the orchard.

YASHA   The old boy won't be there now, he's gone. (*laughs*)

LIUBOV (*slightly annoyed*)   And what's so funny? What have you got to look so pleased about?

YASHA   It's that Yepikhodov, he's a complete hoot, you know. A dolt. Catastrophe Corner!

LIUBOV   Firs, if the estate is sold, where will you go?

FIRS   I'll go wherever you tell me to go.

LIUBOV   What are you making faces for? Are you ill? You should be in bed, you know.

FIRS   Oh yes! (*smiling*) Me go to bed, and who's going to wait on your guests? Who's going to see to things if I'm not here? There's only me to run the whole house.

YASHA (*to Liubov*)   May I ask you something, Liubov Andreevna? If you go back to Paris would you be so kind and take me with you? I couldn't possibly remain here. (*Looking around, in an undertone*) I don't have to explain. You can see for yourself—this country is so backward, and the *people!* It's so boring here, and the food they give you in the kitchen is disgusting, not to mention Firs wandering about the place muttering his gibberish. Please take me with you!

Pishchik enters.

PISHCHIK   May I have the pleasure, you gorgeous creature . . . of the merest little waltz . . . You're an enchantress . . . but all the same, I'll have my hundred and eighty roubles off you, I will, you know . . . a hundred and eighty roubles . . .

Liubov and Pishchik dance into the ballroom.

YASHA (*softly sings*)   "If you only knew how my heart beats for you . . ."

In the ballroom a figure in a grey top hat and checked trousers can be seen waving its arms around and jumping about; shouts of "Bravo, Charlotta!"

Dunyasha stops dancing to powder her face.

DUNYASHA (*to Firs*) Miss Anya ordered me to dance. There aren't enough ladies to go round, but it's making my head spin and my heart's beating too fast, and just now, that clerk from the post office said something that quite took my breath.

The music becomes quieter.

FIRS What did he say?

DUNYASHA You, he says to me, you are like a little flower.

YASHA (*yawns*) Yokel!

Yasha goes out.

DUNYASHA Like a little flower! To a sensitive nature like mine, it's a lovely thing to receive a tender compliment.

FIRS I can see where *you're* heading.

Yepikhodov enters.

YEPIKHODOV I don't suppose you want to see me, Dunyasha . . . I might as well be some kind of insect. (*sighs*) Life! Life!

DUNYASHA What do you want?

YEPIKHODOV And without a doubt you have a point, possibly. (*sighs*) But looking at it from a certain point of view, the fact is you—how can I put it?—forgive my frankness—you have brought me totally and utterly to a state of mind. I accept my lot—there's something every day, some misfortune or other, and I've been so long accustomed to it, I can even smile at it. You gave me your word, and although I . . .

DUNYASHA Can we discuss this later? I happen to be in the middle of a dream.

Dunyasha fans herself.

YEPIKHODOV Some misfortune every day. But, allow me to put it this way—I meet adversity with a smile, sometimes even a little laugh . . .

Varya enters from the ballroom.

VARYA Are you still here, Semyon? You've got a damn cheek. (*to Dunyasha*) Out with you, Dunyasha. (*to Yepikhodov*) First you play billiards and break a cue, then you saunter about the place as if you were a guest here.

YEPIKHODOV Permit me to say, as clerk of the estate, that you have no right to talk to me like that.

VARYA I'm not talking to you like anything, I'm telling you what's what. You just wander about here, there and anywhere doing nothing—we keep a clerk but God only knows why.

YEPIKHODOV (*offended*) Whether I do or not, or eat or play billiards, I only take orders from those in authority over me.

VARYA How dare you talk to me like that! (*exploding*) Who do you think you are? I don't need your say-so about anything! Clear out of here, get out!—now!

YEPIKHODOV (*cowed*) I must ask you to express yourself in a more ladylike manner.

VARYA (*beside herself with rage*) Get out! Out!

Yepikhodov goes toward the door, with Varya behind him.

VARYA (*cont.*)   Catastrophe Corner! I don't want to see you or smell you.

Yepikhodov goes out; his voice is heard the other side of the door.

YEPIKHODOV (*off*)   I'm going to lodge a complaint!

VARYA   Come back and say that!—

Varya grabs the stick that Firs has left near the door.

VARYA (*cont.*)   Come on then—come on—I'll show you— come and show your face—!

Varya swishes the stick just as Lopakhin enters.

LOPAKHIN   Deeply obliged!

VARYA (*angrily and sarcastically*)   Oh, I do beg your pardon!

LOPAKHIN   Think nothing of it, I beg you—humbly grateful for the warm welcome.

VARYA   Oh, please don't mention it.

Varya moves away, then looks around.

VARYA (*cont.*) (*softly*)   I didn't hurt you, did I?

LOPAKHIN   Not at all, nothing to worry about. The bump will be enormous but don't concern yourself.

Voices can be heard in the ballroom. "Lopakhin's arrived! Yermolai Alekseevich."

PISHCHIK   You're a sight for sore eyes and music to the ears!

Pishchik exchanges kisses with Lopakhin.

PISHCHIK (*cont.*)   And you smell of brandy, dear chap, just slightly. We've been having a party here.

Liubov enters.

LIUBOV Is that you? Why have you been so long? Where's Leonid?

LOPAKHIN He's with me, he's just coming.

LIUBOV (*agitated*) Well—what happened? Was there an auction? Say something!

LOPAKHIN (*embarrassed and afraid to show his joy*) The auction ended at about four . . . We missed the train and had to wait till half past nine. (*sighing heavily*) Oof! My head is going round . . .

Gaev enters; in his right hand are his purchases, with his left he wipes away his tears.

LIUBOV Lenya! What's the matter? Lenya? (*impatiently, on the brink of tears*) For God's sake, tell me quickly.

Gaev says nothing in reply to her, only waves his hand dismissively.

GAEV (*to Firs, weeping*) Here, take these, some anchovies and Black Sea herring. I haven't eaten all day. What I've gone through . . .

The door to the billiard room is open; the click of billiard balls can be heard.

YASHA (*off*) Seven-eighteen!

Gaev's expression changes and he is no longer crying.

GAEV I'm terribly tired. Help me to get changed, Firs.

Gaev goes to his room across the ballroom, Firs follows him.

PISHCHIK Will somebody tell us—what happened at the auction?

LIUBOV Was the cherry orchard sold?

LOPAKHIN It was sold.

LIUBOV Who bought it?

LOPAKHIN I did.

Pause.
Liubov Andreevna is crushed; she would fall if she were not standing beside an armchair and a table. Varya takes the keys from off her belt, and throws them onto the floor in the centre of the room, and goes out.

LOPAKHIN I bought it! Give me a minute, ladies and gentlemen, be so good . . . my mind's in a muddle, I can't speak . . . (*laughs*) So we got to the auction. Deriganov was already there. Leonid Andreevich only had fifteen thousand, and Deriganov went straight in with a bid of thirty thousand on top of the mortgage. I see the way things are, so I take him on. I bid forty. He bids forty-five. I bid fifty-five. He's going up in fives, you follow, so I go up in tens . . . and that's how it finished. I bid ninety thousand over and above the mortgage, and the estate was knocked down to me. The cherry orchard is mine! It's mine! (*gives a loud laugh*) My God, ladies and gentlemen, the cherry orchard is mine! Tell me I'm drunk, I'm out of my mind, tell me it's all a dream . . . (*stamping his feet*) Don't laugh! If my father and grandfather could rise from their graves and see what happened today!—how their Yermolai, their beaten, half-literate Yermolai who ran barefoot in winter, how that same Yermolai has become the owner of the most beautiful estate on God's earth! I've bought the estate where my father and grandfather were slaves, where they weren't allowed into the *kitchen*. I must be asleep and dreaming—it's the dream of some deep dark imagining.

He picks up the keys.

LOPAKHIN (*cont.*) (*tenderly*)   She threw down the keys, she wants to show that she's no longer in charge around here . . . (*jingling the keys*) So be it.

The orchestra can be heard tuning up.

LOPAKHIN (*cont.*)   Ho—let's have some music. You're all invited to watch Yermolai Lopakhin take an axe to the cherry orchard! Watch the trees topple! Everything must go! We'll build summer cottages and our grandchildren and great-grand children will see a new life here . . . Music! Play the music!

The music plays. Liubov has sunk down onto a chair and is weeping bitterly.

LOPAKHIN (*cont.*) (*reproachful*)   Why didn't you listen to me? Why? My poor love, you can't undo what's done. It's gone. (*in tears*) Oh, if only all this could be over, and we could start our miserable, messed-up lives again!

PISHCHIK (*takes Lopakhin aside and whispers*)   She's crying . . . Come into the ballroom, she needs to be on her own . . . Come on . . .

Pishchik takes Lopakhin under the arm and leads him into the ballroom.

LOPAKHIN   So what's going on here? Play the music so I can hear it! Let's have everything the way I want it. (*ironically*) Make way for the landlord, the new owner of the cherry orchard!

Lopakhin accidentally bumps into a small table, and nearly knocks over the candelabra standing on it.

LOPAKHIN (*cont.*)   Don't worry, I can pay for everything!

He goes out with Pishchik.

There is no one in the ballroom or the drawing room except Liubov, who sits completely huddled up, weeping bitterly. The music plays. Anya and Trofimov hurry in. Anya goes up to her mother and kneels down in front of her. Trofimov stays at the entrance into the ballroom, watching.

ANYA Mama! . . . Mama, are you crying? Dear, kind, beautiful Mama, bless you, I love you so. The cherry orchard is sold, it's gone, that's true, but don't cry, Mama, you've got your life to live, and your pure, innocent soul. Come on, let's go away, let's go together! We'll plant a new orchard, lovelier than this one, and then you'll see, and understand everything. A deep calm happiness will fill your breast like the sun at evening, and you'll smile again, Mama! Come on—let's go, my dearest, let's go.

CURTAIN

ACT FOUR

The setting as for Act One. There are no curtains at the windows, or pictures. A few pieces of furniture remain, stacked up in one corner as though for sale. The emptiness is palpable. Near the door to outside, and at the back of the stage, suitcases and bundles, etc. are piled up. On the left the door is open, and from there the voices of Varya and Anya can be heard. Lopakhin stands and waits. Yasha is holding a tray with glasses filled with champagne. In the entrance hall Yepikhodov is roping up a box. Off stage at the back, can be heard the murmur of voices of peasants who have come to say farewell.

GAEV (*off*) Thank you, brothers, I thank you all.

YASHA The villagers have come to say goodbye. Peasants have their heart in the right place in my opinion, they're just a bit thick.

The murmur of voices dies down. Liubov and Gaev enter from the entrance hall. She is not crying but is pale, her face trembles and she is unable to speak.

GAEV You gave them your purse, Lyuba. You mustn't do things like that!—really you mustn't!

LIUBOV I couldn't help myself! I just couldn't!

They both go out. Lopakhin goes after them.

LOPAKHIN (*in the doorway*) Won't you please join me in a drink before you go? Please? I didn't think to bring any with me and they only had one bottle at the station. Please do!

Pause.

LOPAKHIN (*cont.*) No?

66

He moves away from the door.

LOPAKHIN (*cont.*)   If I'd known, I wouldn't have bought it. Well, I shan't have one either in that case.

Yasha carefully puts the tray down on a chair.

LOPAKHIN (*cont.*)   You might as well have a drink, Yasha, help yourself.

YASHA   To us on our way! And to those left behind! (*drinks*) It's not real champagne, I can tell you that much.

LOPAKHIN   Eight roubles a bottle. (*pause*) It's damn cold in here.

YASHA   They haven't lit the stoves. Well, so what?—we're off.

Yasha laughs.

LOPAKHIN   Why are you laughing?

YASHA   Sheer happiness.

LOPAKHIN   It's October outside, but still sunny like summer and not a breath of wind. Good building weather.

Lopakhin glances at his watch, speaking through the door.

LOPAKHIN (*cont.*)   Just to remind you all! We have to set off for the station in twenty minutes! You'd better hurry things up a bit.

Trofimov in an overcoat enters from outside.

TROFIMOV   Isn't it time we were going? The horses have been brought round. Where the devil are my galoshes. They've disappeared. (*in the doorway*) Anya, I can't find my galoshes!

LOPAKHIN And I have to be on my way to Kharkov—I can get your train. I'll be in Kharkov for the winter. I've been hanging around here too long doing nothing. I hate not being busy. I don't know what to do with my hands, they look so odd without anything to do, as though they didn't belong to me.

TROFIMOV We'll be out of your way soon, and you'll be able to resume your many profitable activities.

LOPAKHIN Help yourself to a glass.

TROFIMOV No, not for me.

LOPAKHIN So you're off to Moscow?

TROFIMOV Yes, I'm going to see them off, and tomorrow to Moscow.

LOPAKHIN Yes, I expect the professors won't have given their lectures yet—they'll be waiting till you get there.

TROFIMOV Well, it's nothing to do with you.

LOPAKHIN How many years is it that you've been studying?

TROFIMOV Try to think of something original—that one's been done to death.

Trofimov continues to look for his galoshes.

TROFIMOV (*cont.*) Look, since we'll probably never see each other again, do you mind if I give you one piece of advice to take with you? You wave your arms about too much. Try and break the habit, all that arm waving. Also, all the talk about building cottages, and working out how many summer visitors you'll turn into settlers and smallholders—boasting and calculating—that's a kind of arm waving too.

Still, I like you anyway. You've the hands of an artist, and the soul of an artist, too.

LOPAKHIN (*embracing him*) Goodbye, then, my dear chap. Thanks for everything. Let me give you some money for the journey, in case.

TROFIMOV What for? I won't need it.

LOPAKHIN But you haven't got any.

TROFIMOV Yes, I have. Thank you anyway. I got paid for a translation. I've got money in my pocket. (*anxiously*) What I haven't got is my galoshes!

VARYA (*from another room*) Here!—take the smelly things!

Varya throws a pair of rubber galoshes onto the stage.

TROFIMOV What's gotten into you, Varya? Anyway, these aren't mine!

LOPAKHIN Last spring I planted three thousand acres with poppies, and I've already cleared forty thousand roubles on them. They were a picture when they were in bloom! What I'm trying to say is, I made forty thousand, which means I can afford to make you a loan, so I'm offering it. Don't give me that look. I'm just a peasant, I don't dress things up.

TROFIMOV Your father was a peasant, mine had a chemist's shop. It means nothing.

Lopakhin takes out his wallet.

TROFIMOV (*cont.*) Put it away. You can offer me two hundred thousand and I still wouldn't take it. I'm a free man. The stuff that rich men and beggars hold in such high regard hasn't the slightest power over me, it may as well be thistledown blowing on the wind. I can get on without you, or go by you, I've got my strength and my pride. Mankind is moving on to a higher truth, toward the greatest possible happiness on earth, and I'm in the front rank.

LOPAKHIN Will you get there?

TROFIMOV I will. (*pause*) I'll get there or show the way to those behind.

An axe can be heard striking at a tree in the distance.

LOPAKHIN So—goodbye. Time to go. We may turn up our noses at each other, but life goes on regardless. The only time my mind is at peace is when I work nonstop for hours at a stretch. Then I feel I know why I'm here. How many people in Russia exist without knowing why? Well, perhaps that's not the point. I gather Leonid Andreevich has taken a job at the bank for six thousand a year. He won't last, he's too lazy.

ANYA (*in the doorway*) Mama says would you mind not cutting down the cherry orchard till she's gone.

TROFIMOV Well, of course not! You could have had more tact.

Trofimov goes out through the entrance hall.

LOPAKHIN I'll go and stop them, you're quite right, it's a good point . . .

Lopakhin follows Trofimov out.

ANYA Have they sent Firs off to the hospital?

YASHA I told them this morning. They must have done.

Yepikhodov crosses the room to Anya.

ANYA (*to Yepikhodov*)   Semyon Panteleevich—will you go and ask if Firs has been taken to hospital?

YASHA (*offended*)   I told Yegor this morning—you don't have to ask them ten times!

YEPIKHODOV   Our ancient Firs, in my considered opinion, is beyond repair. He should be with his forefathers. I wish I was.

Yepikhodov puts a suitcase down on a hat-box and squashes it.

YEPIKHODOV (*cont.*)   What did I tell you! Uncanny!

He goes out.

YASHA (*jeers*)   Catastrophe Corner!

VARYA (*in the doorway*)   Have they taken Firs to the hospital?

ANYA   Yes.

VARYA   So why didn't they take the letter for the doctor?

ANYA   Tsk! I'll get it sent on after him.

Varya goes back in. Anya leaves.

VARYA (*from the room next door*)   Where's Yasha? His mother's come to say goodbye to him.

YASHA (*waving his hand dismissively*)   That woman would try the patience of a saint.

Dunyasha has been busying herself among the packing all this time; now that Yasha is alone she goes up to him.

DUNYASHA   You might look at me, just for a moment, Yasha. You're going away . . . you're leaving me . . .

Dunyasha starts to cry and throws herself on his neck.

71

YASHA There's nothing to cry about. (*drinking champagne*) In six days I'll be in Paris again. Tomorrow I'll take my seat in the express and off we go, in a puff of smoke. I can hardly believe it. Vive la France! This place doesn't suit me, I can't live here, and there's nothing I can do about that. I've had my fill of ignorance. (*drinking champagne*) What are you crying about? Well-behaved girls don't make a fuss.

Dunyasha takes out a little mirror and powders herself.

DUNYASHA Write to me from Paris. I really did love you, Yasha, I loved you so! I've got a sensitive nature, you see.

YASHA They're coming.

Yasha busies himself around the suitcases, softly hums.

Liubov enters, followed by Gaev, Anya, and Charlotta.

GAEV We ought to be going. There's not much time. (*looking at Yasha*) There's a smell of herring coming from somewhere.

LIUBOV We've still got ten minutes before we have to get in the carriages.

Liubov looks around.

LIUBOV (*cont.*) Goodbye, old house, old grandfather house. Come the spring, you won't be here anymore, they're going to pull you down. What these walls have seen!

She embraces Anya fervently.

LIUBOV (*cont.*) My treasure, your eyes are shining, sparkling like diamonds. You're happy, aren't you, so, so happy?

ANYA Yes, I am. It's a new life starting, Mama!

GAEV (*gaily*) She's right. Everything's going to be all right now. Until the cherry orchard was sold we were all so worried and worked up, but once the question was settled once and for all, everybody felt calmer, you could even say quite cheerful. I work for the bank now, I'm a financier. Yellow into the middle. And you're looking better, Lyuba, you really are, inspite of everything.

LIUBOV Yes. My nerves are better. It's true.

She is handed her hat and overcoat.

LIUBOV (*cont.*) I'm sleeping well. Bring my things, Yasha. It's time. (*to Anya*) Darling, we'll see each other again before long. Paris here I come, with great-aunt's money she sent to buy the estate. Here's to her! Well, it won't last long.

ANYA But you'll come back soon, won't you, Mama? You will, won't you? I'll study hard and pass my exams and then I'll go to work, so I'll be able to help you. We'll read all kinds of books together, Mama, won't we? (*kissing her mother's hand*) A wonderful new world will open for us. (*to herself*) So come back, Mama.

LIUBOV I will, my darling.

Liubov embraces Anya.

Lopakhin enters. Charlotta begins to softly hum a tune.

GAEV Charlotta's happy. She's singing.

Charlotta picks up a bundle resembling a swaddled baby.

CHARLOTTA Bye-bye, my baby . . .

The baby's cry is heard: wah, wah.

CHARLOTTA (*cont.*) Hush, my little baby boy . . .

The baby is still crying: wah, wah.

CHARLOTTA (*cont.*) My poor baby!

Charlotta throws the bundle aside.

CHARLOTTA (*cont.*) So I'm counting on you to find me a place. I can't stay here.

LOPAKHIN We'll find something, don't worry.

GAEV Everyone's deserting me. Varya's going away, suddenly nobody needs me.

CHARLOTTA I've nowhere to live in town. I'll have to move on. (*hums*) Well, so what?

Pishchik enters.

LOPAKHIN Look what the wind's blown in, "Fancy That" himself!

PISHCHIK (*out of breath*) Oof—let me get my breath. I'm exhausted. Dear friend, a glass of water!

GAEV On the scrounge again, I suppose. No disrespect, I'm getting out of the line of fire.

Gaev goes out.

PISHCHIK Quite some time since I was here. You're as enchanting as ever. (*to Lopakhin*) You're here, too? Delighted to see you. A man of enormous intellect. Here, take this.

He hands Lopakhin some money.

PISHCHIK (*cont.*) Four hundred roubles. That leaves eight hundred and forty I still owe you.

LOPAKHIN (*in disbelief, shrugs his shoulders*) Somebody pinch me. Where did you get it from?

PISHCHIK Tell you in a minute. I'm boiling. A most unexpected occurrence. Some Englishmen turned up on my property and found some kind of white clay on my land. (*to Liubov*) And four hundred for you, you beautiful, wonderful woman. (*he hands Liubov some money*) The rest later. (*he drinks some water*) There was a young man on the train who was saying that a great philosopher advises us to go and jump off the roof. "Jump!" he tells us. There's no problem it doesn't solve, he says. It's his whole philosophy in a nutshell. (*astonished*) Fancy that! More water.

LOPAKHIN What Englishmen?

PISHCHIK I've given them a twenty-four year lease on the part with the clay. But now, forgive me, time's up. I must trot along. I'm going to Znoikov's. And to Kardamonov's. Owe them all money. (*he finishes his drink*) Cheers! I'll drop in on Thursday.

LIUBOV We're moving into town in a minute, and tomorrow I'm going abroad.

PISHCHIK What? (*alarmed*) Moving to town? Oh, I see. So that's why the furniture! And the luggage! Well, never mind! (*on the brink of tears*) Never mind. Extraordinarily intelligent, these English. Never mind. Be happy. God be with you. Never mind. All things come to an end.

He kisses Liubov's hand.

PISHCHIK (*cont.*) And if you hear that I've come to mine, spare a thought for this old, this old horse, and say, "There once was a man called Simeonov-Pishchik, God give him peace." Most remarkable weather. Quite.

He goes out in a flurry, but returns immediately to speak from the doorway.

75

PISHCHIK (*cont.*)   Dashenka asks to be remembered.

Pishchik goes out.

LIUBOV   Now we can go. I'm taking two worries with me. There's Firs who isn't well. (*glancing at her watch*) Perhaps we've got five minutes.

ANYA   Mama, they've already taken Firs to the hospital. Yasha sent him off this morning.

LIUBOV   And I'm worried about Varya. She's used to rising early and getting down to work, and now with nothing to occupy her she'll be like a fish out of water. She's got thin and pale, and she's always in tears, poor thing.

Pause.

LIUBOV (*cont.*)   You know what I'm saying, Yermolai Alekseevich. It was my hope to see her married to you, indeed things looked to be going that way.

She whispers to Anya, who nods her head to Charlotta and they both go out.

LIUBOV (*cont.*)   She loves you, and you—you feel something for her, and, I don't know, I don't know, but it's as if you two are determined to lose each other. I don't understand why.

LOPAKHIN   Nor do I, I must admit it's all very strange. If it's not too late, I'm ready to propose to her. So let's settle it, get it over with—*basta*. With you gone, I don't think I'd ever get around to proposing.

LIUBOV   Good! It'll only take a minute. I'll fetch her.

LOPAKHIN   It just so happens there's some champagne.

Lopakhin looks at the glasses.

LOPAKHIN (*cont.*)   No there isn't. Someone's had it all.

Yasha coughs.

LOPAKHIN (*cont.*)   Siphoned it up.

LIUBOV (*animatedly*)   Excellent! Out we go. Yasha, *allez!* I'll call her. (*in the doorway*) Varya, leave everything, and come here. Come along.

Liubov goes out with Yasha.

LOPAKHIN (*glancing at his watch*)   Yes . . .

Pause.

There is restrained laughter behind the door, whispering, and finally in comes Varya. She spends some time checking the luggage.

VARYA   That's strange, I just can't seem to find . . .

LOPAKHIN   What are you looking for?

VARYA   I packed it myself, and I've forgotten where I . . .

Pause.

LOPAKHIN   What are your plans now, Varvara Mikhailovna?

VARYA   Me? I'm going to the Ragulins. I've agreed to look after things for them, be their housekeeper, I suppose.

LOPAKHIN   That's in Yashnevo, isn't it? Must be forty or fifty miles away. (*pause*) Well, this house has come to the end of its life.

VARYA   Oh, where can it be? Perhaps I put it in the trunk. Yes, life's over for this house. All over.

LOPAKHIN And I've got to go to Kharkov now, on the same train. Lots to do. I'm leaving Yepikhodov in charge here. I've taken him on.

VARYA Really?

LOPAKHIN This time last year the snow had come, do you remember? But this year it's sunny and calm. Cold, though. Three degrees of frost.

VARYA I didn't look. (*pause*) And anyway, our thermometer is broken.

Pause.

A voice is heard through the door from outside: "Yermolai Alekseevich! . . ."

LOPAKHIN (*as though long awaiting this summons*) I'm coming!

Lopakhin goes out quickly.

Varya sits down on the floor, rests her head on a bundle of clothes and sobs quietly. The door opens and Liubov cautiously comes in.

LIUBOV Well? (*pause*) We have to go.

VARYA (*stops crying and wipes her eyes*) Yes, it's time, Mama. I'll get to the Ragulins today, so long as we don't miss the train.

LIUBOV (*in the doorway*) Anya, put your things on!

Anya enters, then Gaev and Charlotta. Gaev is wearing a warm overcoat with a hood. The servants gather, and the drivers. Yepikhodov fusses around with the baggage.

LIUBOV And now we can be on our way at last.

ANYA (*joyfully*) On our way!

GAEV My dears—my dear friends and loved ones! We're leaving this house for the last time. How can I remain silent, how may I not express at this moment of parting, the feelings which fill my entire being at this—

ANYA (*imploringly*) Uncle!

VARYA There's no need, uncle!

GAEV (*despondently*) Yellow—off the cushion—into the middle pocket . . . I am silent.

Trofimov enters followed by Lopakhin.

TROFIMOV So, come on everybody.

LOPAKHIN Yepikhodov—my coat!

LIUBOV I'll just sit for one more minute. I never took the slightest notice of the walls and ceilings before, and now I want to look at them forever, they break my heart.

GAEV I can remember being six years old one Trinity Sunday, sitting by this window watching my father going off to church.

LIUBOV Have we got everything?

LOPAKHIN Looks like everything. (*to Yepikhodov, putting on his overcoat*) Make sure you keep everything in order, Yepikhodov.

YEPIKHODOV (*speaking in a hoarse voice*) Count on me, sir.

LOPAKHIN What's happened to your voice?

YEPIKHODOV I had a drink of water and I think I swallowed something.

YASHA (*with contempt*) These country bumpkins!

LIUBOV We're leaving, and there'll be no one left . . .

LOPAKHIN Until the spring.

Varya pulls an umbrella out of a bundle, as though about to brandish it at someone; Lopakhin makes a face as though taking fright.

VARYA What's the matter with you? It was the last thing on my mind.

TROFIMOV All aboard, ladies and gentlemen. It's time now. The train will be in soon!

VARYA Petya—there are your galoshes—they were behind this bag, (*on the brink of tears*) and look at the state of them.

TROFIMOV (*putting on his galoshes*)   Let's go!

GAEV (*distressed, frightened of bursting into tears*)   Off to the train . . . the station . . . In-off into the middle pocket, white off the cushion into the corner pocket . . .

LIUBOV Come along!

LOPAKHIN Are we all here? No one missing?

He locks the side door on the left.

LOPAKHIN (*cont.*)   There's some stuff stored in here, need to lock it up. Let's go!

ANYA Goodbye, house! Goodbye, old life!

TROFIMOV Welcome, new life!

Trofimov goes out with Anya.

Varya casts a glance around the room and unhurriedly goes out. Yasha, and Charlotta with her dog, go out.

LOPAKHIN Well, that's it, till spring. Come on everyone. Goodbye!

He goes out.

Liubov and Gaev remain alone together. They may have been waiting for this moment, and they collapse on each other's necks, sobbing quietly, afraid that they might be overheard.

GAEV (*in despair*) Oh my sister . . . sister . . .

LIUBOV Oh, my poor, sweet, lovely orchard! My life, my childhood, my happiness, goodbye! Goodbye!

ANYA'S VOICE (*cheerfully, calling*) Mama!

TROFIMOV'S VOICE (*cheerfully, excitedly*) Hallooo . . . !

LIUBOV One last look around at the walls . . . the windows. Mama used to love this room.

GAEV Oh, sister, sister.

ANYA'S VOICE Mama!

TROFIMOV'S VOICE Hallooo!

LIUBOV We're coming!

They go out.

The stage is empty. The sound of a key locking all the doors and then the carriages can be heard leaving. It grows quiet. Amid the silence the dull thud of an axe against a tree, rings out solitary and sad. Steps can be heard. From the door on the right Firs appears. He is dressed, as always, in a jacket and white waistcoat, with slippers on his feet. He is ill.

Firs goes up to the door, tries the handle.

FIRS Locked. They've gone . . .

He sits down on the divan.

FIRS (*cont.*) Forgot all about me. Never mind. I'll have a little sit down here. And Leonid Andreevich, I'll be bound, hasn't put on his fur coat, gone out in his light overcoat, (*sighs*) I never looked to see. These youngsters.

He mumbles something which cannot be made out.

FIRS (*cont.*) My life's gone by as if I never lived.

He lies down.

FIRS (*cont.*) I'll just lie down for a bit. No strength left, you haven't, you've nothing left, nothing. Ekh, you . . . noodle.

Firs lies motionless.

A distant sound, as though from the sky, is heard, the sound of a breaking string, dying away, sad. Silence descends, and the only thing to be heard, far away in the orchard, is the thudding of an axe against a tree.

Then the distant sound of the train approaching.

CURTAIN